Walking the Animals

CAROLA LUTHER was born in 1959. She grew up in South Africa and moved to England in 1981. She works in Leeds and lives in the Yorkshire Pennines.

CAROLA LUTHER

Walking the Animals

CARCANET

First published in Great Britain in 2004 by
Carcanet Press Limited
Alliance House
Cross Street
Manchester M2 7AQ

A CIP catalogue record for this book is available from the British Library
ISBN 1 85754 767 5

The publisher acknowledges financial assistance from Arts Council England

Typeset in Monotype Bembo by XL Publishing Services, Tiverton
Printed and bound in England by SRP Ltd, Exeter

For my mother and my father

Acknowledgements

Versions of poems in this collection first appeared in the following journals: *PN Review*, *Smiths Knoll*, *Pennine Platform*, and the South African journal *Carapace*. Thanks to the editors.

Thanks also to Carol Ann Duffy, editor of *Out Of Fashion* (October 2004) for which the poem 'Nineteen Thirties Suit' was written.

For their encouragement, advice, comments and support, thanks to Olwen May, Tim Moss, Jenni Molloy, and above all, thanks to Sheila Kershaw.

Poems in the sequence *Searching for the Point Marked X* include phrases or words from the following verses of the King James Bible: Ezekiel 9.2 ('Census'); Isaiah 54.1 ('Neither breaking into song nor crying aloud'); Jude 1.16 ('Departure'); Deuteronomy 13.5, 22.5, 23.1, 23.2 ('Departure'); Ezekiel 19.10 ('The Mother Idea'); Job 42.17 ('Full of Days').

Contents

Walking the Animals

What the buddha saw

Walking the Animals

Walking the Animals

She lets out her animals down by the canal
when no one is looking. Opens the hinged
ribs under her coat saying *come on now*
sweethearts, out you come, come out quickly!

It's the giraffe she has trouble with, his neck
or his shin getting stuck in her throat,
but she hopes he'll unfold to a canter
and there'll be no vomiting. The parrot

and the carp, nippy little twisters, can tie
her in knots with their double-act around
the toes of the wordless rhinoceros
but she's not daft, she keeps her eyes

on his horn. How light she is, she has to hold
onto the branches when the cacophony starts.
What holds her attention is the fury of the midges
and the lonely way the buffaloes shake

the ground. As ever, the crippled dog howls
for his liver which was stolen at birth, accounting
for the wastes of his eyes. The sound never fills him
but makes a drone for the shrieking snakes

to rail against, the delusion of frog song, the cheetah's
weeping. Inevitably there are complaints
from frightened walkers, but they don't stay away.
Ignoring them, she hangs on tight to the afternoon

until she has coaxed the little grey bird from its hollow
and launched it westward over the water
to pull its reflection to the point
it ignites in the silence of the setting sun.

Mourning

When I am hopeful I see
there is not much difference
between a rock and a rhino
that a rhino is warmed-up stone
that stone is tight water
that water is wind
coloured-in.

When I am hopeful I see
there is not much difference
between giraffe and green trees
that trees are slow thoughts
that thoughts are quick fish
that fish are loose flecks
of river-light running
and rivers are longing.

When I am hopeful I see
there is not much difference
between a lion and warm wood
that wood is slow flame
that flame is lit sand
that sand is dry sea
that sea is wet sky
that sky is still mountain moving
from where I can reach
and touch you.

Landing near Halifax

I know this sky. Its runnels, channels
thickets, its thorns of ice. The drop
to the moist grey mounds, the hiss
of space. I lean on an easterly, ride
its lithe spine. I watch the earth
slide round its stone. I await my exit

trail fingers in light. I could roll up
that stream, make ammonite.
Or hang that road over a stick
slack as milked snake. But I take
the descending spiral. The fall
is quick. Mass. The pull of my feet.

What I have come from shrinks, a gap
between hills. Weather swarms.
Wall looms. Furrows fill. A field
full of sorrows. Here it rains, weight
on my hair, wet on my face. I land.
Feel the stones grow in my space.

Pull

Few angels visit now. They've moved
inward and starward, and finally dropped
the myth of wings. I miss them. They brought news
of my gaudy sister and other planets.
They were gentle. Their feet did not press
my pale powder or disturb the pocks of my face.

Since the landing, I too have put up my defences.
Her men breached my deceits. They laid weight,
punctured my pallor, stole my wan stones. I
have been measured, had small suns shone
into my most intimate bruises. Their detritus
continues to gather. The dark is tense with its spinning.
Its shadows make my scars ache.

I want to shut my eye, finally close
the last white slit, and turn away. What do I care
if her vivid hips tilt? Or that on her side
her iris would stare at the frozen dark
while one cheek burned? I am betrayed

by the terror of my own absence. I am grey.
My dust is livid with desire, my envious eyelid cold.
I have to concede, I cannot drop her.
She remains my lit, warm, blue jewel. I cannot
take my eye off her. She breathes.
Her skirts eddy about her roundness. She responds
to my longing. Her colours shift. Green. Yellow.
Violet. Blue. The fading angels know what I mean.

Compass

Not gulls, magpies, pigeons, crows.
Those dots between chimneys
are swallows arriving from Africa.
There is the trance in their eyes

the pull of poles, the aching hope
of plenty, insistent instruction
of absolute stars, the pillions
of winds, of winds, the long

leash of light, of shadow. Surrendered
as sea to the moon, bewildered
still by the cosh of the desert,
the ocean's unceasing moan, the swallows

know nothing but yearning
for home, a barn west of Leeds
where they'll rest and grow
fat again, where they'll breed,

feed on flies, nest, swoop
and sing, pretend to be
bats, and finally give in
to that other compass of longing:

the south, the south, the south.

Architecture

Cars have had their lights on all day.
The valley is a smudge except for the shine
on plastics. Trees look like losers.
The river is preparing for something
full of unpleasant thoughts. Walking
to town she sees a dead fox. No message
in its entrails, it's not that open.
Where the fur's ripped, is meat
neatly bunched in a wrap of silvery muscles.

She is disturbed by the ear. Alert as a candle
it seems to listen, each hair separate,
attentive as frost. A diversion of skin:
another ear tiny as that of a mouse.
She follows its fjords down through a hollow,
onto the bony curve of a path turning in always,
climbing down and down into the gathering
grasses, the tunnelling dark. A roof
opens. Expanding cathedrals of sound.

Collecting Light

The last brown beech-leaves shine
their little lamps in the dusk. The sun didn't
rise from its mist today. Lit cars come and go

each raising a neurosis of leaves from the gutter.
Fog coils along the darkening valley, sliding
its belly along the river's wet back.

The old man with the accent is heading for home.
The house with smoke in a column to the cloud
is his, he doesn't use smokeless

because *where is the flame*, he says. Yellow glows
in his window every day the sun
doesn't shine. Today he's been collecting

a smooth wet stone, copper wire, a rosy toadstool,
a glove (cerise), a new wet plank, a rosehip
(red), a rosehip (orange), a see-through orange

plastic bottle without a label, and held
in his mind the moments of breakthrough
bleeding on the bruised sky to the west. *Still alive,*

he repeats to himself in his own language,
placing his feet carefully within dim yellow pools,
the torch of bright beech held high in his hand.

Her Hair is Discouraged by Millennium Static but Christmas Remains Red and Green

Station Road. She feels the night growing glass,
hears it splinter minutely. Norland Road. The stars
are clean. Water Street. With vicious mathematics
they take their positions, give signs. Bridge Street.
The tarmac glints, there will be accidents. Wharf Street.
An ice this minute takes root, cracking the fields
for tomorrow. Rochdale Road. She remembers her soul
is the sum of her memories, she should not be wasteful.
Rochdale Road. Tomorrow, ponds will be stopped
with thick lenses, grass blades rigid with frost. Rochdale Road.
Nowhere to hide for the frogs. Middle Street. She is afraid
of the calendar, unlooping the delicate grey of her brain.
East Street. The moon's in a skid. Stile Terrace. Planet
without water, it could be an omen twisting there in the air.
Doorstep. The neighbours are shouting. Kitchen. The moon
could also be bits of a saucer flung from a window.

Pros and Cons

I watch the coloured roofs of six-inch cars moving,
and on the top floor of the tower block I understand
it is over. I still haven't thrown away the typewriter
or the copper Impala clock made on the Witwatersrand.

The pros had been the sky, the tops of trees. *Loving*
takes more than a middling view – I heard this often
but it didn't sink in, though we agreed about the kidney bowl
gleam of the lift, and the bleached beige landings. (Softened

I thought, by homely touches, for example the landing on eight:
personally, I loved the cactus and poster of the desert sunset
but here we differed.) The morning that she told me, she dropped
her coffee in her rush to get ready, staining the velvet

pyjamas I'd got her for Christmas. Being late
for work had always upset her so I carried on typing
beside the poinsettia with my wine gums and tea, thinking
Must clean up that coffee, get rid of that clock. Later, citing

the cons, she packed. The Impala yes, the fourteenth floor
yes, that fucking typewriter clacking away like an antique
loom yes, next door's bastard screaming baby, the doomed poinsettia,
the communal drying area, or rather the suicide launch deck

yes, floors so cold they could fridge dead bodies, the door
of the lift wheezing like illness, the so-called balcony,
the ten-stair monotony, the wine gums, the filth beneath bleach –
but all these she could live with. It was me. It was me.

A faint lapping like water followed her, the random hissing
of cars. I watched the sky, the tops of trees. Someone knocked
saying would I sign the petition even though it was done
and dusted already, sewn up, stitched, end of the line for our block

and what were my plans anyway, now it was up for demolition?
I said nothing, chose the red wine gum, started hoovering.
Wet washing was smelling. Out here by the line, I think
of the clock, the typewriter. Follow the colours of small cars moving.

Explanation

There is an animal amongst the children.
When we are busy, they pass it along their line.
Their faces concentrate on things other
than the scuttling across their palms.
When one of us looks up, they become still,
then move their arms avidly,
whistle, and examine the sky. We cross
the ditch, restore order uniformly.
Nothing is discovered. But in the silence
we see it move across their eyes.
There is an animal amongst the children.

The Ringing of Breakable Things

Today you can run your finger around the rim of the sky
and it will sing clearly for you in glassy blue. The trees
will harass your eyeline: they are cocky with inner sprouting
and pose athletically like cats. All is well. Your iris is awake
in the sun, your pupil plumbs the precision of things
with telescopic panache, and your lens curves perfectly
parallel to the blue curve of earth. Yet there's too much
ringing in things. Tonight you'll dream

of the dam where water is narrow, banks steep
and ringed like wood, scoured with the dispossessions
of drought, each scar a notch of loss, a brown tide
of sinking. Yet crocodiles have crossed land for this place.
Laboriously, at night (when at times of disgrace, darkness
must do for a river). You don't see them. You assume
they have withdrawn down into themselves, recouping
in the depths. The waiting of water is unbearable.

April 1999

A swarm of silent white landed
in April, took the farmhouse somewhere
like Poland, dropped it on an old-fashioned hill.

It could have been war. The lanes were black
with columns of stones, like heads
intent on reaching a border, any border

between winter and colour, spring a figment
of frippery slipped to the west, reality
a utilitarian, ancient, carapaced thing. Snow

focuses the eye on what is not white
on walls, what is dead, what is burned, what is empty
or tightly shut to survive. Bulbs burrow deeper.

What They Took

Boxes of goods, electrical, unopened.
Two Hoovers, three portable
stereos, a television, a caravan
fridge. Selvete took the curtains
donated by Cross Street Methodist Church,
though they hadn't the weight to keep
out the dark. Flamur took a drill,
a saw, a cigarette rolling machine,
his Motorola phone. Beside himself
on the NHS wheelchair with *St David's
Hospital* printed on the back, Valdrin
took an Action Man still in its packet,
a tape he'd made of Remi singing,
some Pokemon cards, the card that said
they'd all had tetanus, polio, TB
and three HepB jabs, and the certificate
that confirmed his diagnosis. Remi
took the photos of Alban and Dwayne,
and a close-up of Jenny who met them
off the plane from the camp
in Macedonia. Hava took some tattoo
transfers, the new Nike cap Kelly
had given her, a small paperback
dictionary, and condoms, secreted
under Kelly's address. The twins
took all the toys donated by the people
of Hull that they could carry, Sala
took sweets in a tin, her new false teeth,
several boxes of tampons, knickers,
three for two pounds from the market.
Mehmet took five dozen Elvis winking
lighters, and a golden ring for Sala's
thirtieth birthday. Blerim took books.
Sevdije took clothes for the children,
the travel documents and the money
in a wallet round her neck, needles, cotton,
Valdrin's medicine, gloves for Valdrin,
a little box from Boots containing plasters
and antiseptic, and in a yellow bag,
all the painkillers and sleeping pills
she had saved from the doctor's prescriptions.

Keepsake

for S.M.K.

Whether it was the wind, blustering and aggressive, lifting
your hair from the curve of your face, or the backing up of clouds
of deepening grey in the west, whether the heron opening up
its silent width of silhouette had something to do with it,

or my thoughts about an eel swimming, as I watched the river slip,
whether the sliding of incessant muscles brought me to the phrase
you don't step into the same river twice, or to the hint
of anxiety I felt as I dug over the onion bed, whether perhaps

it was the reappearance of the sun, the pale slant igniting the reds
in the wooden slats of the shed, or the way the powdered light
fell upon your skin, as you sat at rest, perfectly composed
within the rosy uprights of the doorway, or how you looked up

and smiled as I turned to wave before going up to the house
with the newly planted seed-trays, whether it was the tenderness
of that smile, or just that I saw it, saw something lit
solidify like amber around you, and wanted to hold it,

to hold it, to pocket it before water covered my eyes and blurred
what I was seeing, so that I needed to move back to you instead,
surprising you by pulling you up into my arms, and holding on to you,
not lightly, not as if I never would have to let go of you again.

Fifth

The man painting railings
does not notice the sky
drop a notch for winter.
When he looks up
he sees it hanging
above his face.

He walks home with the care
that comes from living
in a low house. Summer
has finally sunk its yellow
into the canal. A duck drills through,
leaves a path like a skinny brown ribbon.

The man will find a fire
tonight, let the dark explode
in momentary orange.
Then he'll click shut
the fastenings of his anorak
and prepare for the cold walk home.

A sail,

tense, you curve in between the moon
and the lids that protect us.
You fly your shape

precisely over my stones, or over
my neighbour's, while the sleepers
in our arms remain fields of warm coriander.

All day we feel you coming – a woman
watches the west, as if waiting for a wake
of geese, a man interrupts

his friend in the pub
to thank him in bursting words.
You swerve towards us. The tension

in trees, horror ringing through water,
barns skirting the haggard hills.
We hear sound like windmills.

Feel the pull of the boats
that we dream on. The coldness,
dropping. The shiver of a hovered wing.

Earth

On nights when dreams hollow out her bones
and the dark plumb rolls from her heart
and the wind from the steppe slides under the doors
lifting her body like an untethered shirt
or the cross of a kite that cartwheels the sky
or a plastic bag in a storm
or an empty scarf that startles the grass
or a ghost, a gasp, a moon

the woman beside her shifts in her sleep
and circles her wrist with one hand
holding on all along the runway of night
over the sound, the gulf, the bight
the badlands, the wetlands, the shantytown heaps
till the light brings them back in to land.

Functions of Fish

Most breathe water, using the little
ruffled skirts round their cheeks
to tease out oxygen. Take the gills
of hagfish. All damp pleat and frill
and veiled fold, to be rolled
and unrolled like rows of little Rizlas.

Lost in mudslums, others breathe air,
amia, pantoden, lepidosiren.
These are frontierfish, the voortrekkers
of evaporating dams. They use scale
or hindgut for breathing; they stop
at nothing. Megalops, polypterus,

lepisosteus, they reach for amphibia,
and guard the secret of swimbladder.
Blown from a twist in the foregut,
these pockets are lung, drum,
waterwing and tympanum. They listen,
they sing, they breathe, they keep

our fish afloat, while echoing
down the aeons to the very beginning,
in case we must crawl from water again.

Under Cover

If he stopped holding on to himself,
opened his mouth and let opinions clatter
to the floor in the sudden silence, the slit
and far yellow gaze of something like goat

would slip over the eyes of visitors
sipping their tea, he would feel himself lift off
for safety, tether adrift, the string of a childless
balloon, see the house, the city shrink

to the size of a biscuit, damp little fields
spread to the edge of the map of England,
see Ireland, Scotland, France, the sea shifting
this way and that in its groove, trace the blue

curve, sun escaping the rim, night seeping along
the hem of the hidden woman walking abroad,
and the bluer the marble the quieter
the shadowless light, and Africa

yellow and green pinned down by tiny white
Kilimanjaro, slipping away, Ethiopia first
like the wing of a bird, America coming
over the Atlantic, earth reduced to a coin

in a spin, the moon a white shriek indignant
behind him, so he must turn and encounter
its mouth, and land face down in a basin of talc,
close-up close-up, the bleached, stale absence.

He'd move. Eventually. His lips. His eyes.
Make an angel with his arms. Wonder
how long he'd manage this time, to remain
undiscovered. Moustachioed. In disguise.

Silver

Thin. Hard. Cool. Of high
altitude. Of dark-eyed miners, coca
mountains scraped blue,
ozone and time. Precious
but not that precious. Of money
the passing of money, the arts
of bright-fingered androgyns of love
and circuses. Handsome,
scored, nicked, the bewitching
smile of trickery mixing
with desire. Irretrievable. Irresistible.
Of long thumbs and slow hips

silver is not for wedding rings.

Narcissus

Nothing could tempt him except the thing
that he glimpsed like a glint in an other
like a twist of a fish in a river, the glance
of a sliver of silver or mirror in the eye
of a stranger who could be a lover
of men or of women, or just glisten
with thinking of swimming.

Narrowboat

We picnic in the buzzing summer
gaze, doze
watch the slow grasses passing.
Unexpectedly the canal begins to quicken.

I know little about narrowboats
but here I am sailing your long green home with you
and you it turns out
know nothing.

Anyone can feel
there is too much longing in the water.
It is drawn to its horizon which should not be getting nearer
but it is.

Suddenly rushing
it appears we are heading for a weir.
It falls like a mouth full of teeth
into riverine rapids.

There is no time to discover how exactly you managed this
but I am too young for drowning.
While you sit rooted I throw the tiller
and lean all my terror and will on it.

I don't expect it to work.
Unlike you I have never done anything of use
so this is surprising
that your narrowboat

on its very edge
juddering against the cables of currents which pull
while I push
slowly, so slowly, actually turns.

Now we chug into the fan of our wake.
Summer is buzzing.
Nothing might have happened
except we stare without words at each other

I who know little about narrowboats
you who know everything else
but about narrowboats, you will have to concede
you know nothing.

The day before war the sun

lies on the field quiet as cloth.
If the wind blows, it blows gently
leaving no trace of itself in the grass.
Shadows stretch out reflecting
black wing-tips experiencing blue.
Sun like hands upon the field.
Quiet hands, washed, soft as cloth.

Occupation

There he is acting as if he owns the place. Swaggering
over the land all hip and thigh, pale as sea-meat.
Terror has hardened, I have hidden myself in a nest
of stones. Soon I will be able to move. When the sun falls
at an angle, I will stand up and walk. I will

cross the enclosure as if I'm about to collect the eggs
for his meal. I will lean down, exposing the bone of my back
to his gaze. I will drop my shadow over my hand,
my good fingers parting the dirt, the broken
awaiting their turn. I have rehearsed the turn.

When the moon is folded in smoke, I practise the rise
and twist of sickle and claw, until it is smooth as dancing.
Waiting for sleep each dawn, I keep out the ache
for escape, with a picture of mocking cut short, a meal
interrupted, astonishment widening sky-colour eyes.

Odds

She had only to think of the migrants,
the people taking turns in the kapok
dark to place their mouths over air-
holes bored through the floor of a crate;
those who would follow the black stretch
of shadow of the walker in front over days
of hot yellow rock stacked up in blocks
or tipped like cities; those in the cracks
who darted through ruins, avoiding orphans
with guns or flies in swarms, searching
for signs of unmeasured roads to railways,
planes, to ferries, to lorries, to container
ships; the threads and scraps of a dither
of butterflies staggering south, just above
waves like a wisp of blood or a ragged
handful of leaves on the sky or a snatch
of bright song torn from a singing mouth.

Genome

The morning is a pale egg. News
through the night reported on wars
and the project naming our parts. I open
the door. Soon my desire will be protein,
success again a shred of hereditary meat.

A cat sleeps in the garden, joints pulled under
its orange cosy. Mist moves, drugged cows
shift at the gate. When I pass I will stare
till I find the lost kudu in their milk-whelmed eyes.
Someone's stirring in the far house

yellow squares appear at the bathroom window.
Outside, the candles are up on the chestnuts,
the cherry's pink sunk, a yesterday wedding.
A wandering dog crosses the road. A crow gulps.
Buses begin.The nurse comes out from number seven.

What will be the name of his morning cough,
his habit of knotting bags twice for the bins?
There is new blue heat in the grass on the hill.
The function of bluebells, I see, is its pooling.
What may they call the thin dog running

through my sleepless heart? Pale globes
of dandelions balance and wait. Anything could happen
to these houses in their half-sleep. The woman at four
stumbles out with washing and a cigarette. Pegs up clothes
in a secret order. What is the name

of the skin between the small yellow sock and the pink
trouser leg? The overlap of dreams of people in Freetown
and Leeds? Would limbs, lopped, retain the name
of the wounded, or become part of the ownerless dog
lying under a child soldier's tree?

Routes

Strangers came into our midst. Beautiful, disfigured,
poor as chickens. Over the mountains, one by one, running
on the day our computers went up in smoke. Rounded up
in cul de sacs they were taken to enclosures, and the word
put out that links were obvious. The clacking of the train
from the capital came and went, a plane took off for America.

I could see the fence from my tree. Guards every few yards,
clerks behind slanting desks, slow queues moving.
Papers were piled. Passports, address books, letters of love,
of recommendation, scanned, recorded by hand, burned.
Sky shrivelled. Smoke rose and hung. The sound of the train
from the capital came and went, and a plane flew in from America.

Trucks were loaded. Khaki and black, packed with ragged
strangers they dispersed down roads, over the plains to the withering
east, the west, the northern erosion. Red dust rose and hung.
Trucks diminished to the size of beetles. In the silence I still heard
songs, leaping and tumbling in unknown registers. The train
from the capital came and went. A plane took off for America.

Dreaming of Birds

She unclipped the spawn of the digitalbit
and discarded it. Felt celltime accelerate,
strange lappings of hormone. When the street-eye
clicked, she slid her feet off the mobile path
and walked, as she had learned to do in history
fields of the park. Despite pain, she transgressed
customer responsibility contracts, and headed
for the sunk estate. A nanoman detained her
saying 'Madam, for your own good...' She broke
for danger. Once across the pale, she felt sweat.
She had not imagined sensations of crumbling spine

or risk unsupervised. Naturals watched from space
between shelters. Despite preparation, their lack
of symmetry shocked her. Some gazed, one cursed
in true English. She asked the way. Struggled
to follow their directions, her mother's tongue
being marketing. But she recognised the ruin
of factory they spoke of, skirted an old singer,
a disused interface, a group fingering books.
She knew when she found it: writing on wood
said *Garden.* Writing on metal said *Toxic
Keep Out.* She opened the gate to growth.

Plants like darkstockinged legs accosted her.
Twines with long tongues nested and stroked
and stung her. She twisted past bones, burnt
bits of things, found a bell, a letter in Romanian.
She followed the sounds of water. Removing
her clothes, she lay, feeling the certainty of clods,
their cold surprise. Turning to the sky she saw
clouds unframed. Watched their changes till dusk.
Imagined birdsong. Then hanging her arms
in the water, where poisoned ribbons of moon
swam close to her eyes, she sang herself to sleep.

valentine

that feeling
that spring will be possible
that feeling
that somewhere like cuba
is contained in the fringe
of the wind from the west
that the atlantic is thinner
and almost pacific and there's heat
in the way you sashay the kitchen
as if sun is syrup on your hips
that while trees are still ashen outside
and the light on the pennines is fine
as rings of pale wine in cold glasses
the rhythm on the radio leads to us kissing
and your tale of learning the importance of tipping
the head to the side so that lips and not noses
collide and the anxiety about choosing which angle
when practice was only with mirrors not men
and the only solution being the recruitment
of nina your friend whose lips were wide and dark
and surprisingly warm and able to bend and her taste
remained in your mouth reminding you of something
between sleep and the sea and how much you yearned
and learned including that worrying about which way
to tip so that lips and not noses collide when you kiss
is a waste when pawpaws and mangoes are hidden inside
the puddles of sun in even a wintry kitchen and salsa is waiting
to swing from beneath the most regular beat of a radio drum.

Nineteen Thirties Suit

Hassock and tussock, and lake by night, my lining
sliding around the inside white of your arm.
Hidden in the smell of man there is the farm,
the obstinate animals (let go, let go and settle
down, their steam, the hay is warm, is kind,
their dreams a nudge, a pushing down
the blissful mud, the sup). Get up.

Tonight we're clean, my crease pressed
hard along your length of thigh, keen
with intention like mind, like money, comfortable
you, high on your legs, your fine leather shoes,
my tweed holding and falling in folds,
in pleats, in darts from waist, from hips,
smoothed over arse, and the swinging skirt

of a jacket lifted, pocket, waistband, steady,
worsted, gathering together the cocky white starch
of your shirt. We arrive at the door. I softly turn
your thoughts to peppers, orange and green,
remind your blind tongue of its search for pips in the pear,
draw your attention to cups, the drop of tulips
half-closed and demure in a turquoise vase.

You appraise the poise of a woman full to the brim
in her skin, the wide cascade of that frock,
the way it sways its dark-red bell (she's the belle
of this party), introduce the idea of light
you might find in a fuchsia tent, imagine going down,
going under, the bowl of skirt outside like a gentle house,
while beneath, in here, the secret life of thighs.

Waiting for the Goatherd

Thus curtailed, he folded his clothes,
collected the laptop and identity
papers. There was nothing for him here
now the orange blossom had dropped
to the ground. He no longer felt drunk

in the scented moonlight, found himself wanting
salt on a freezing wind. She had not come
for the pomegranates he'd ordered
on the Net from Iran, nor had she touched
the bolt of silk though it shivered

on her doorstep like a night-time
river. Predictions were not heeded.
Farmers ignored Himalayan possibilities
traced on his spreadsheet, and her brothers
continued to harvest traditional beans.

He left a note, bitter with brevity
and the pips of immaculate English,
then hitched a lift to the nearest airstrip.
A plane tomorrow said the man
at the gate. Yes. He would wait.

Laying out raisins, he made letters
of his name, played solitaire and improvised
patience. He counted out lovers, failures,
addresses, spelled out her name both forwards
and backwards, and finally ate the raisins.

No plane the next day into the country,
no plane out. On the road a goatherd
stopped in a 1973 Mercedes.
A stone was tossed. Landing the way it did
meant war in the north the young man said

and offered him his bottle of Fanta.
He would give him a lift to the south
in return for the Ted Baker shoes. The road
ahead was full of craters, its edges converging
in mirage. The sun rang like tin

on the ringing road, and trees in the heat lost
focus. He thought of the uptown street
where his mother lived. Imagined it weeping
with rain. The goatherd spoke of the sadness
of his brother's guitar, and saving up

for England. The animals were slow.
Soon to be killed, the goatherd said. Meat
for an important wedding. The car stalled,
and hoping for oil, the goatherd went
searching, carrying a billy-can into the dusk.

The passenger seat was unhelpful. Outside
were goats, the hot bump of skulls in the dark
like sons pushing up at his fingers. He shuffled
between beasts till they were all around him,
till he was up to his thighs in their river.

Feeling absurd and blessed he decided to sing
and stroked the goats with sorrowful hands.
Then sucking a mint for the thirst, he lay down
to rest, and warm in their pungent shifting,
he waited for dawn to quell the rupture of stars.

Waiting for Rain

Down where the river is
a child is dreaming of swimming.
There's the dry red hip of the bank
and no water
but still it's cool as a bubble of shade down there
and the deep green smell of the oil and the river-pump's mutter
make of the shade a place of dreaming.

The child picks snails from the rock.
They are smaller than fingernails
and eaten with concentration.
Behind her and up where the sun is
a man chops wood.
He has cracked feet and forgetting eyes
and his shadow is dense and short in the noon.
How loud the heat in his ears –
the drought has shrunk the breadth of the earth
and quietened even the monkeys.

The man chops wood and waits.
The child is dreaming of swimming.

Collision

Approaching from the east, having passed where motorways divide
like the arms of a dancer, going south to cities, or north to where geese
without shadows split lavender sky and simplify into lines of intent
direction, approaching fast from the east in the empty dawn, I saw her
there,
standing still in the middle of the road as if watching the sky fill up

with that peculiar and intimate light that belongs to linings of organs
or the wet inner surface of shells, the trembling colour of membranes
moist with life exposed, standing there transfixed with the event of this
particular morning, as if for that second nothing mattered at all except sky
or the way the light was gathering colour to a point of anticipation,

like someone awaiting the impact of a distant explosion and for some reason
I thought of the river of my childhood rising, as if I were watching floods
from the Drakensberg mountains swell the dry river bed I knew to be dry
to the extremities of a different completion, and the stones I stepped on,
the stepping stones I used to run on, jumping beneath the dark

green canopy of leaves that sounded like water in the dry yellow wind
of the lowveld, so the idea of river survived even through the longest years
of drought, because sound was there to imagine a river in, pouring down
from the trees like floods from mountains and filling the space, the sand
between rocks, and this I was watching, that moment, that morning,

the brown waters rising, darkening the rocks and the pale stones
I stepped on, the stepping stones darkening in the impossible
eddying movements of water alive and climbing, and the diminishing
crowns of stones I knew like planets, like summits, like craniums
sinking and the white bubbles streaming up were thoughts, rushing

like urgent geese in lines from the mouths of stones as if the stones
were drowning people, the pressure of thoughts intense and unbearably
precious in the quietness of that dawn, approaching from the east
as I was, towards the figure standing still in the middle of the motorway
watching the perfect timing of morning the moment before we touched.

Searching for the Point Marked X

Census

We are afraid. A man in a pale linen
suit has come to our town, his ledger
and quires loaded onto a government
donkey. In the other pannier, is a folding
table and chair, ink in squat bottles, indigo,
carmine, sepia, jet, a selection of nibs
and a fountain pen set in a velvet box.
We see him moving towards noonday
houses with his silent companions.
It is the muscled companion who knocks.

Each day my uncle returns for his meal
covered in dust. *Has he come?* he asks,
and my sister mouths *No* from the shadow
of the well and my mother continues to wash.
At night I keep watch while my brothers
come up from the earth. *Is he come?* they ask.
I shake my head and feel the darkness tighten.
My first brother drinks with his face
in our mother's hands, *I am not frightened
Ma*, he weeps, *I am not frightened.*

My second brother's eyes are stones, he
is used to the dark. He draws diagrams
in the dust, and when he is ready, tattoos
them in code onto the planes of his body.
My uncle sweeps the floor clean. My brother
oils and re-oils his gun. My uncle sweeps
the floor again. By dawn, they are gone.
Food is less. My mother grows thin.
My sister rehearses me for an hour each dawn.
I learn my new name. It is noon when they come.

Good day says the man clothed in linen.

Departure

Give thanks. You too have been found
to be righteous. Laughter is not appropriate
boy – murmurers have been excluded,
prophetesses, and those known to be lying
with one on the list. Cross-dressers, women
with pillows, bastards, people who have eaten
on mountains, those wounded in the stones

cast out. We're a narrow crowd, yes. Keep
your mind on the last ochre pass. Think
of the desert, of reaching the sea. They are not
so different. Sand moves slower, tricks you
with silver. But neither have drink in the flint
of their rocks, and the danger in both
is illusion. Distance is unknown. Stop dwelling

on the leader. Watch your feet, my heels
in front of you, mete out the minutes in steps.
Hold the dewy cloth to your mouth in the mornings,
cover your head in the day. Sleep within the shadow
of your rock during the hottest hours, move
only when necessary, and avoid the eyes
of the leader. Never think of your mother

or that wanton boy. The allocated women
will be godly, and in time we may find we are glad
of their company. They too will have sorrows
behind their veils. Remember the laws
of cleanliness and once a trust has been built,
ask your woman to wake you if you are beginning
to dream. I cannot keep this vigilance up

alone. You will eventually learn to sleep
in silence. Stop crying. There's no point
asking what happens when we reach the sea. I can't
imagine even its colour. Pick up your bundle
son, the juniper staff I made you. Please.
Forward. Look forward. Stop searching
for the boy. Your mother has stopped waving.

Neither breaking into song nor crying aloud

we stand and look at them. Most of us thin
but not all. We stand and look with barefaced
absence, hair pulled back, tight under cloth

unanointed, unadorned, awaiting conclusions.
From a distance our faces may resemble eggs
of different colours. Our robes are all the same

grey, the colour of concrete, of sullen clouds. Skin
they insist, must be covered, except for our hands.
Swagger or suggestion meet not with wrath

but disappointment, though the most brazen amongst us
elicit disgust. No, not the old days, no fingers
broken, no one drowned or burned or lamed

but questions remain. Are we formed, finished,
damaged, whole? Are we stopped, half-grown,
arrested, ignorant of the oldest human secret

our salt an ever-running river, a scar of primal
failure, our act of blocking helices, ladders
from dark to light, from death, from entropy to life

pulled up, pulled up, is blood betrayed, who forgives,
can they, the unborn swimming in abandoned pools,
the thrusting trunk of evolution, the science-sacred

root and branch and little beads and leaves of carnal
purpose lit like candles, can ancestors, who begat, who
begat, can the womb, the moon, the brute, the mothermind?

We stand and look at them. They think of herons, cranes,
migrating geese. We stand and stare with barefaced
absence, hands strong, hair covered with cloth, grey as rain.

Companion

Now the sky has fallen, who will find us and take us home,
you with your bloody nails, my concealed shadow and I? The beloved
elder has done his duty, went out ahead to beat a path to somewhere,
but now is out of reach of voices. The line south lies unmuscled,

dead as a snake. We must stick together, hold hands, hang onto poles
and trees, marking them with something durable as we move through fog
towards the equator, where we have heard there is no pull at all
and rocks must be put into shoes and pockets to hold us down

until the tropics, where you can be sure my shadow will emerge
all innocent, as if it's been sleeping like a pale baby,
but even in the doldrums it'll be tugging and ragged and trying
to fly away, fiddling and fiddling on its own violin, demented, enraged

with the rope at my ankle, flapping its rags like a scrap on a wrack,
waving for help at the absent wind, as if disaster had already happened
which it has but not that, this will last longer than pieces of string.
I should (but find that I can't) stand you crying. Your wounds in the heat

I'm sure will scab over. We'll prepare well for the flies and the ants,
make improvised whisks of vine, or sisal. We may even find honey
for healing and bitter fruit to stop you eating your hands. Let me lead
for a while. I'm afraid, but I can see better than you, here in the north

and just knowing you are there is comfort. Think of the moon
and our violet mountains, the stars shattering like glass, the orange fire
coiling down to the plains, and scrawled on the dawn, the ibis. Imagine
that's where we're heading. And if you stand

on my shadow when you see it, pinning it down, and if we wrap
your hands in leaves of some description, and if we walk
where we haven't walked before, and if you could please stay alive,
we're sure to make progress of a kind, in one direction or another.

Crossing

Pitching was worse than rolling. The berth
was shoulder-width and with the dying of the lights,
the darkness, like a coffin, reeked of piss.

Wood veneer was what I knew. A knot
and whorl of alder, fake, close up, the line
not quite aligned, where two strips met.

Then the lights went out. Silent Barnabas
began to speak, to Mary, to St Anthony, and cried
out when on all fours, I started for the upper deck.

What I couldn't stand was the random way
he'd press his watch, so the pale green light
would illuminate its little circle, his chin, his neck

the snowscape of the twisted sheet, his face
at any moment. *Barnabas*, I said, *do you want to fight?*
It made no difference. I made myself a bet

he'd ignore requests to count ten Mississippis.
Proved right, I said, *Barnabas tell me, is it spite*
or madness, your arbitrary unmeasuredness, and hit

him. The stain had spread across the snowdunes
when he pressed his watch again, moonlight
green and ghostly, prayer like fever. It was then I left

on hands and knees, marvelling even in the pitch
black corridor of lurching bodies, at my tight
control. Someone vomited on my head.

Turning back towards the reedy light
I thought, *Barnabas, you're dead.*

The Point Marked X

We spent a long time searching for the point
marked X on the map before concluding
it was another country. It had rained
for days and the ink had run and our hands
were covered in the blood of giant mosquitoes.
Go north said Freeman, *beyond the highlands*

to where nothing breaks the expanse
of snow except oil and chromium diggers.
Samira snorted. *And gun towers guarding the fence,*
and rank upon rank of assassin! A taint
of despair was staining the air and I knew I'd be alone
when I woke, the wrong map and cold remains

of the fire my possessions. I did go north. Where else,
now the east and the west were chronicled
and the south reduced to bone. I felt a need in myself
for something to reach, a hill perhaps, a river.
My arms and legs were oozing mosquito
poison, I shook with rigor and blackwater fever.

It is hard to remember the reality of the Pole
when everything is white and the compass swinging
in circles, or lurching from left to right. To recall
at this time the passionless way you chose your goal
is unhelpful, to concede its randomness, death. You're alone:
your nose must be followed, a rhythm set up, a cheerful

version of your repetitive heart, your muffled feet.
Sound must be made in the powdery absence of sound,
you must converse with yourself, enthuse on the route,
pretend it's not luck that today you weren't food
for the wolves or the petrol bandits, picture mosquitoes
to remind yourself how bad it might be, conserve heat

by holding your skin away from your jacket,
not let yourself think that the corpse that you pass
might be the corpse you saw before, or that the socket
belongs to the eye of someone you know, instead
let your mind rest on a purpose for travelling alone
in endless white, and reach for a path in your head.

The Mother Idea

We examined canyons, searched the firmament.
Attention was paid to narrow pits, ditches
deep and shallow, waterholes, wells, and eroded

channels between stubble and tenements
abandoned in the wastes. Rats and matches
were needed for sewers. Once, in a cave, air exploded

stringing potholes together like sudden yellow beads
underground, burning shadow, X-raying glory
on the hidden arts of stone, then returning

us bereft to blindness. Some settled, sowing seeds
of restlessness amongst adopted children, telling stories
to sheep on drunken hillsides. There were other warnings.

An elder disappeared. Found near death in a ruined zoo,
lying with rifle among the lions, crying that arms were always
empty. Someone murdered. Another walked into the sea.

Still we searched, some with faith, however secretly. Who
we were, we could no longer say, but on good days
we felt fast and free scouring the mountains, trees

understood our whisperings, and we saw what was coming
in petroleum pools. Now sometimes the poor thank us
for the news we bring them. We still look in furrows, moats,

silt formerly used as winelands. We wade in fields swimming
in liquid, drag marshes, swamps, unpoisoned rivers,
pick our way through overgrown fish farms. Boats

are used in lagoons to dive from. Like a vine in our blood,
the mother idea remains fruitful and full of branches. It is food
of sorts. All we know is it's planted by waters, roots in mud.

Legend

Ancestor knew of at least one who made it to the lip
of the crater: her name meant spring. What she had
was steadiness of limb, a strong back, and belief
that each step mattered. She kept watch like a thief
and held on to the seedling through the thick

and thin of it, through smoke, collision, furnace
fire, through meteor, sulphur, magma, dust
the blast and counterblast of shale and scree
step at a time, step at a time, in her mind a tree
green and sweeping, to be planted by her calloused

hands on arrival at the summit, to grow
from this tender double-tongue of cotyledon
watered by her spit, shielded by her hands
protected by her back from the fire-wind's
suck, the hot hail of cinders. Progress was slow

each level of the gyre another twist of knowing
the volcano. There were times she despaired, once
she almost let herself fall forward into the pit's
lost heart, pulled by the serenity of unlit
finality. She often staggered, slipped. Allowing

herself a little pity, she would gather her limbs
and wits, check her tiny tree, spit, and move on
again. Then the moment she saw the colour blue
through the red haze above her, how the new
leaves seemed to shiver, and something far within

burst through her, so tears ran from joy, from terror
making mud about her and salty little rivers. Then
the stone of having still to put one burned foot before
the other, the sudden ton of seedling, borne
like a child, an ailing lover, the impossibility of the last heave over

the blackened edge, the branches in her mind the only levers
left to move her, lift her, swing her and her little tree
out of there forever, *and she did it* said Ancestor.
*And the tree grew green and sweeping by the waters
of her weeping, green beside the mountain…*

Full of Days

The map is less vital, the nearer the coast.
These serve well as a compass:
kelp-wind and sea-fret in from the east;
hurried no longer, river through mist
spread out like a fat silver thigh; the west
where the light dies last, opposite
the noise of the swarm, herring gulls
calling to war. Living by their wits

men with tattoos and their backs to the hills
scan the flats of the sea for ships
and porpoises, fillet occasional mackerel,
search for sole, or lines, or ballast
for pining boats, spend whole nights out
in force four gales with brandy. This
tells us where we are. Ready for another bout
of living, we make camp. Shellfish

scavenged from rocks on the fire, the sound
of sea to sleep to. And being kissed
on a whim by a warm-armed woman, a wave
of summer, of hope, of happiness
drifts in, and from the cliffs next day, the haze
of grey, and the clarity of blue begin
to feel of almost equal value; the way we may change
is glimpsed; and how, if the edge, the rim,

the coast is always close, we could practise being full of days.

What the buddha saw

What the buddha saw (I)

The buddha sits on his green plinth. Sees the fury
of the purple crocus opening beside daffodils. Sees sunsets
and a lawn with square holes for roses, sees the sky scudding
distracted past the privet hedge. Behind the house's red
edge, a branch, a half trunk of cherry tree, sunk in pink,
pink dropping, pink sinking on the green, a wedding
dress stepped out of, a wedding finished. And twice a day
the coming and going of the tight man, this way, then that way.

From the street, Jamila sees a magpie sit on the buddha's head,
watches it poke its beak beneath a wing where the smallest
feathers must lie packed, stacked like wet scales;
sees the buddha's head, bald and pale, facing the garden
away from her on the street. The magpie lifts off,
clicking its wire feet. Liane says 'Hey Up.' Jamila smiles.
They enter the warehouse, sign in, check mail, tease Lester Jack.
Through the office window, Jamila looks at the buddha's round back.

In the break, Lester tells Jamila he'd do anything if dared.
'It's my personality,' he says, while Liane raises her eyes
to the ceiling and Soraya shakes her head. 'OK Tiger,'
Jamila says. 'That buddha in the garden opposite. I dare
you to turn it round.' 'What do I get?' asks Lester Jack. 'No kick
in the butt,' says Liane. 'A little less flack.' Next day the figure
of the buddha smiles straight into Jamila's eyes.
'Thanks Lester,' Jamila says. At dinner she buys him banoffi pie.

The buddha sits on his green plinth. Now sees the dawn
whitening the east. Watches the gravel leading to the gate
in the concrete wall, and the black shoes of the neat man going,
his neat shod feet coming back. Watches the ivy
growing up the wall, and pink flounces landing on the path.
And then there's the woman, knowing
what she knows, watching him through the window over the street
smiling at his stone smile, at his tummy, resting on his stone feet.

What the buddha saw (II)

A line of ants on the ridge of the garden wall.
The scorch of eczema on Jamila's hands on the wall.
The dream that lifted her skin last night and burns
beneath. *The mother escaping a town to the desert,*
the powder and bone of the shattered desert, the mother's hands
emptied by soldiers who chiselled a son from her grasp,
the twisting spoon of her unborn, repetitive feet in the dust.
The decreasing distance between ants and hands on the wall.

The pink of Liane's new hair as she joins her friend by the wall.
Her chin between bitten-down cherry-red nails on the wall.
The workers behind walking towards their morning shift.
The chimneys above them sponged by moving clouds.
The dream dropping inward as Jamila spots Liane's hair. Hands
up to her mouth, then back to the wall. Liane's eye winking,
her sideways smile. Jamila's delight at bright pink hair,
the column of ants approaching her hands on the wall.

Liane looking at the watch on Jamila's wrist on the wall.
Puzzled by a thought of desert in the reddened hands on the wall.
Looking up at the face that watches the buddha. Puts an arm
round Jamila. Steers her to work. And the ants pass by on the wall.

What the buddha saw (III)

The shadow of himself
slimming, the shadow
of himself and his plinth

stretching, a tall thin
buddha, a buddha with a neck
reaching, touching

climbing the wall. Distracted
by the people walking,
people leaving work,

the warehouse door
swinging open, swinging
shut, there Jamila

pointing, laughing
a young man running,
a woman with pink hair

flaming, yelling 'Toe-rag!
Git! I'll get you Lester Jack.'
And Jamila passing

with her friends,
passing by, and forgetting
to look back.

On the gravel
balanced, a Ripple
wrapper, silent

the quiet lawn,
the gravel,
the wrapper

and the wall.
The gate that swivels
on its hinge. Gravel

that shifts beneath
the sole of one shoe
then the other,

the creasing and the smoothing
of black shoe leather,
the tight man

returning home.
Gravel. Ivy. Settling
fly. A blue car

passing. Chimneys. Sky
pale and far. Three seagulls, letters
of the alphabet. Long, pulled

shadow of the plinth
nearing the ridge of the wall.
Sun setting

in the warehouse windows,
filling up the empty
windows, orange panes,

orange squares, orange,
orange, copper polished
gold. The shadow of the buddha

tipped. Off the wall. Lost.
The budhha's lit back.
His face. Lit.